Talking Eagle
and the
Lady *of* Roses

The Story of Juan Diego
and Our Lady of Guadalupe

Written by Amy Córdova with Eugene Gollogly

Illustrated by Amy Córdova

SteinerBooks

ong ago, in a small village in old Mexico, a baby boy was born. A child of the Great Eagle Clan, he was named Talking Eagle, *Cuauhtlatoatzin*, in the language of his people, the *Nahuas*.

Talking Eagle and his family grew corn, beans and squash on their little patch of land. When Talking Eagle wasn't hoeing and digging the good earth, he helped his father weave sturdy sleeping mats made of the maguey cactus.

The villagers all agreed that Talking Eagle fit his name.
He was a kind boy and a dreamer of visions, and like the eagle,
he could rise above and see things that others could not.

He loved to wander alone among the hills, and was always
the first to greet the dawn, to find the newborn fawn in
its secret resting place and the first tender green sprouts of
springtime.

In the dew dappled light of early morning, before the
scorching summer days began, Talking Eagle gathered
the wild and glorious roses of *Castilla* that dotted the hillsides
near his village.

Whenever a neighbor became ill or sad, Talking Eagle was there to give comfort. From the little pouch he wore around his neck, he took healing herbs, *remedios*, and made a tea that would soon bring the sick person back to health and happiness.

Talking Eagle grew to be a fine young man.
He fell in love with a kindhearted girl from his village,
and he asked her to be his bride.

Many years before, from the faraway land of Spain, men in long robes, who called themselves Brothers of St. Francis, came to the land of the *Nahuas*. They brought with them the lovely roses of *Castilla* that now bloomed on the hillsides, and they told wondrous stories of the Son of the Great Creator, the one they called the Lamb, who gave his life to save the people of the Earth.

The holy stories etched deep and vivid pictures in Talking Eagle's mind. Talking Eagle and his wife became faithful followers, and they received new names that would mark their place in the flock of the Lamb. Talking Eagle became Juan Diego, and his wife became Maria Lucia, Mary of the Light, in honor of the blessed Mother of the Savior.

The years drifted by, and like the sweeping changes of the seasons, they brought changes to the world of Juan Diego and his good wife. Maria Lucia went to heaven with the angels, and Juan left his *ranchito* to take care of his old uncle, *Tio* Juan Bernardino.

Every morning Juan Diego awoke with the sun, put on his *tilma*, his cloak made of cactus fiber, and headed out to walk many miles over the rocky hills to hear the sacred stories of the long-robes and to pray.

On this December morning, snow laced the high peaks. The icy wind had a snapping bite. Juan felt the cold air clutch at his bones. He folded his arms tightly inside his *tilma* to keep warm. Overhead, a lone eagle spiraled in the blue sky.

As Juan rounded the little hill of Tepeyac, he stopped short in his tracks. He rubbed his eyes in wonder. "What a funny old man I am. The years are playing tricks on my eyes!"

Above the hill, to the east, lingered a glowing cloud arched by a shimmering rainbow. The delicate scent of roses filled the air, and sweet songs of summer birds surrounded Juan and filled his head. So delicious was the scent, so enchanting and bright was the singing that Juan became dizzy with joy.

But then something else made Juan's eyes open wide. He heard someone call his name!

From the cloud before him appeared a radiant young woman, dressed in a flowing gown the color of wild *Castilla* roses. Around her delicate shoulders and head, a *rebozo*, a shawl, the resplendent turquoise of the *quetzal* bird, flickered with the sparkling stars of heaven. Her long hair glistened black as onyx stone. And, most astounding of all, her skin was the color of warm, brown earth, just like Juan's.

Behind her, streaming golden rays of the sun illuminated her magnificence. All around, the rocks and plants glimmered in miraculous rainbows and delicate hues of spun gold.

In a voice that can only compare to how angels must speak, the beautiful Lady called to him.

"*Juanito, Xocoyote*, my dear little son, you are my messenger to the leader of the long robes, the bishop. You must tell him to build a house of prayers on this very hill, so that in it I may show my love, my mercy, my help and protection to you and to all people who call on me in their sorrow."

Juan's feet flew like the wings of an eagle. His heart was a wildly beating drum when he arrived at Bishop Zumárraga's house. But the bishop and his helpers were very busy, and Juan had to wait and wait, many long hours, for his chance to tell the bishop of the magical Lady and her request.

Finally, Bishop Zumárraga and his helpers listened, but only half-heartedly. When Juan was finished, they shook their heads at his fantastic tale. Juan Diego, the Talking Eagle, could see most clearly that no one believed him.

And then, like an annoying fly, he was brushed away.

Juan felt the full weight of his failure. His steps were heavy as he returned to the hill where the Lady waited.

"You must go back to the bishop again, Juanito. Tell him it is Mary, the Mother of God who sent you."

"Please, dear Lady, send someone else, someone important, to tell the bishop," Juan sobbed. "No one believes me. I am not educated in their ways. I am a nobody."

"For that very reason, dearest son, I have chosen you. All of my children are precious to me."

Her smile was the light of the rising Sun.

The next morning, Juan awoke with the dawn and set out on the long trail to the bishop's house. He again explained the Lady's request to the bishop. Now Bishop Zumárraga was losing patience with Juan and his incredible tale. He told Juan that proof was needed. If the Lady is truly who she said she is, she must give him a sign.

On his way home, Juan circled the little hill of Tepeyac, and there the Lady was waiting for him. Juan told her the bishop's demand for a sign that would prove to him that Juan was telling the truth. Again, Juan begged her to find a better messenger, one whom the bishop would believe.

The Lady listened quietly to Juan and then told him to return the following day for the proof the bishop so desired.

It was evening when Juan arrived home at last, only to find his *Tio* Bernardino burning with fever. This time, Juan's healing teas had no effect.

In the morning, knowing that the old one was near death, Juan did not intend to visit the Lady as he had promised.

Instead of going up the hill, he hurried toward the village to bring a holy long robe to pray over his beloved *Tio*.

But just as Juan turned away from the hill, there again, appeared the beautiful Lady. "*Xocoyote mio,* my little son, where are you going?" She called to him. "What road is this you are taking?"

Once again, she listened with compassion to Juan's apologies. "Listen, my son, to what I tell you now. Do not fear your uncle's illness. Are you not under my protection? He will not die, as he is well, even now."

(And this was true, as Juan learned when he returned home later.)

"And so, Juanito, now is the time for the bishop's proof. Come, let us gather my roses."

Roses in December? Anyone could see that roses would not be blooming on the mountains in December.

But when Juan reached the hilltop, his astonished eyes were met by hundreds and hundreds of the most glorious, full-blooming roses of *Castilla* he had ever seen!

The Lady gently placed a rose in Juan's *tilma*.

"You must promise to show these roses to no one but the bishop. This is the sign that will bring him the courage to build my house of prayers."

His *tilma* full of the rosy blooms, Juan set off with a heart as light as a hummingbird's feather. He had the Lady's undeniable proof!

As he hurried along the path, he stole a peek, now and then, at his precious treasure, to be sure he hadn't dreamed it.

When Juan arrived at the bishop's house, he was met by the unfriendly stares of the bishop's helpers. The scent of roses filled the air. Aha! The helpers saw that Juan carried something in his *tilma*. Did he have roses?

They tried to force open his *tilma*, but Juan gripped it tightly to his chest. Three times they tore at the *tilma*, but Juan held fast. On the third attempt, they though they saw something melting into colors on the fibers of the *tilma*.

Just then, amid all the noise and confusion, Bishop Zumárraga arrived.

When Juan saw the bishop, he opened wide his *tilma*. Dozens of the glorious, full-blooming roses of *Castilla* tumbled to the ground. And there, on the fabric of his garment, was an image of Juan's Lady, painted in the luminous colors of Heaven. All eyes lifted to her. It was the Mother of God, *Nuestra Señora,* our *Guadalupe.*

With tears streaming down their cheeks, the bishop and his helpers fell to their knees. From that day on, they became courageous and were faithful to her. Most of all, Bishop Zumárraga, who in his secret prayers had asked for the sign of roses.

Over many years, the great church dedicated to *Nuestra Señora Guadalupe* was built by countless hands on the hill of Tepeyac. And it stands there still, as a center of prayers, healing, and hope for all of Our Lady's precious children of the Earth.

AFTERWORD *by Eugene Gollogly*

THE HISTORY

According to legend, in ancient times, the people from Aztlan, the Aztecs, left their homeland in Old Mexico, led by divine guidance to search for an eagle perched on a cactus, with a serpent in its mouth. They found this "sign" in a region of seven lakes, where they established their empire and built their capital city, Tenochtitlan, which would become Mexico City.

When the Spaniards arrived there in 1521, they found a thriving city, but also a religion based on the sacrifice of human lives to Quetzalcoatl, the Feathered Serpent. The Franciscan missionaries came to bring the Christian gospel of love and peace to the natives. Conversion, however, was often enforced at the point of the sword. Bishop Fray Juan de Zumárraga was a defender of the natives. He prayed to the Virgin Mary for help, asking for Castillian roses as a sign that his prayers were heard.

Among the local natives was an Indian peasant who had welcomed the Franciscans and had been among the first to be converted. He had taken the name Juan Diego. To outer appearances he was simply a poor Indian, but his original name, *Cuauhtlatoatzin*, "he who speaks like an eagle," indicates that among the Nahuas, his native people, he was of a noble clan—the eagle, the representative of the Sun god.

As the story was recorded, in the early morning of December 9, 1531, Juan Diego was crossing Tepeyac hill, a sacred place where there had once been a temple to the peaceful Aztec goddess of fertility Tonantzin, "Our Mother." A radiant Lady arrayed with stars appeared before him. She spoke to Juan in Nahuatl. The Lady asked Juan to deliver her message to Bishop Zumárraga, requesting that he build a church on the hilltop in her honor. At first, the bishop was doubtful, and he asked for a sign. Finally, when Juan returned, after many trials, with his *tilma* (cloak) full of blooming Castillian roses and the imprint of Our Lady on its fibers, the bishop realized that this was the answer to his prayers.

The church was built, just as the Lady asked, which was the home for the miraculous tilma until 1976, when the large, modern Basilica of Guadalupe was completed. Outside the old basilica is a statue of faithful Juan Diego, who was canonized in 2002, the first indigenous saint in the Americas. Today, the shrine of Our Lady of Guadalupe is the most visited Catholic pilgrimage place in the world.

THE NAME OF THE LADY OF ROSES

The origin of the name *Guadalupe* has always been a matter of controversy. It is, however, widely believed that it came about because of the translation from Nahuatl into Spanish of the word used by the Lady herself. She is said to have called herself *Coatlaxopeuh*, which means the one who "crushed the serpent" or Quetzalcoalt, the god who demanded human sacrifice. Another story is that the Spaniards named her after the "Black Madonna" of the Sanctuary of Guadalupe de Caceres in Spain, where there is a sixth-century statue of Mary carved in dark wood. Many Mexicans today often call Our Lady of Guadalupe, endearingly, "La Morenita" or "Little Darkling." In 1660, the Roman Catholic Church designated Our Lady of Guadalupe as "the Mother of God," and in 1737, she became the Patroness Saint of Mexico. In 1945, Pope Pius XII proclaimed her Queen of Mexico and Empress of the Americas, from Alaska to Tierra del Fuego—from the Eagle to the Fire.

THE TILMA

The Lady imprinted her image onto Juan Diego's *tilmàtli* or *tilma*, which in those times was usually made of a coarse fabric derived from the maguey cactus, that was wrapped around the shoulders as a cloak or mantle. A normal maguey tilma would naturally decay in about fifteen years, but Juan Diego's original tilma and the image of Our Lady are still in perfect condition after nearly five hundred years. Recent tests have indicated that the fabric is hemp, which is known to last for hundreds of years, but the miraculous image itself remains unexplained by scientific investigation.

OUR LADY OF GUADALUPE TODAY

The Feast Day of Our Lady of Guadalupe is celebrated on December 12.
She is honored throughout Latin America and by Native Americans in the United States who include her among their sacred ancestors in their homes and churches, sweat lodges and kivas. Over the years, millions upon millions of pilgrims have received her healing blessings. Not just an image but a living presence, Our Lady of Guadalupe is the heart of Liberation Theology—the comforter of the downtrodden, the despairing, and the poor. She is called upon today as she has been for centuries as the champion of the oppressed from the Mexican War of Independence to the Caesar Chavez marches in the 1960s for the rights of farm workers and the recent marches for immigration reform in cities across the country.

In sweet memory of Deborah Howell

and to Tanya Vigil . . . shining daughter of Guadalupe

SteinerBooks

610 Main Street, Great Barington, MA 01230

www.steinerbooks.org

Text copyright 2011 by Amy Córdova and Eugene Gollogly

Illustrations copyright 2011 by Amy Córdova

Library of Congress Cataloging-in-Publication Data

Talking Eagle and the Lady of Roses : the story of Juan Diego and our Lady of Guadalupe / illustrated by Amy Córdova ; written by Amy Córdova with Eugene Gollogly. — 1st ed.

p. cm.

ISBN 978-0-88010-719-8

1. Guadalupe, Our Lady of – Juvenile literature. 2. Juan Diego, Saint, 1474-1548—Juvenile literature. I. Gollogly, Eugene. II. Title.

BT660.G8C67 2010

232.91'7097253—dc22

2010032329

Printed in China